ABOUT THIS BOOK

This book was created from a compilation of pearls that were collected during Sanskrit Studies programs with Manorama in 2006, 2007 & 2008.

AUTHOR'S STATEMENT

This book came about after many years of teaching on the subject of Yoga… a vast and often overwhelming subject for students. It is the teacher's job to help the student build the path towards Self one step at a time. Over the years, I have discovered that Self-transformation is best nurtured in small ways and with love and continuity. These teachings, in the form of pearls, reflect that idea… that one step at a time, one moment at a time, one pearl at a time, one can digest the moments of life with awareness, and feel the auspicious transformations that life offers. These pearls are for contemplation. They are to be thought on, and turned around and around in the mind. They are to be laughed at and they are to be sat with silently. It is my great wish that all who read them experience *shantam*, peace and harmony, and that they share that harmony with others.

~Manorama

DEDICATION & GRATITUDE

This book rests on the shoulders of the loving teachers I have had the great privilege to study under, I am deeply indebted to all of them: Herbert Berghof, Uta Hagen, Edgar Garcia, Pt. Birju Maharaj, Dr. R. K. Sharma, George Bailin and Guruji, Shri Brahmananda Sarasvati. There are no words to convey the depth of appreciation and love in my heart for all of the amazing things you all have shown me... all that I can do is bow my head, in quiet reverence and touch your lotus feet.

Special thanks to Brahmani Devi for her invaluable and amazing support on this project. Thank you to Ambika Devi for her skillful and loving support organizing specific sections of the text for greater understanding. Thank you to Vidya Devi for her support with organizing early sections of the pearls.

Thank you to all the dear students who compiled these pearls so lovingly and meticulously over the years.

Special thanks to Jennafer D'Alvia for her fantastic editorial support.

Lokāḥ Samastāḥ Sukhino Bhavantu.

MAY ALL BEINGS EVERYWHERE BE HAPPY & FREE

I. Reverence

1

Make this life a reverent dialog.
The key is how to kick off the dialog.

CONTEMPLATION

_____

_____

2

Start the journey with reverence
and you start with the highest.

C O N T E M P L A T I O N

_____

_____

_____

_____

3

We must make a connection with ourselves
and others through reverence.

CONTEMPLATION

4

The reverent link is the transformative process.
We must always look for that link.

CONTEMPLATION

_____

_____

_____

_____

5

The bridge to grace is reverence.

CONTEMPLATION

_____

_____

_____

_____

6

Find the grace in the process.

CONTEMPLATION

7

We are human beings,
with humanity moving through us.

CONTEMPLATION

_____

_____

_____

_____

8

Find God in every moment.

CONTEMPLATION

9

Share what you see, but with modesty.

CONTEMPLATION

II. Yoga

10

Yoga is the experience of wholeness.

CONTEMPLATION

_____

_____

_____

_____

11

Yogic elegance:
Minimal effort for the maximum result.

C O N T E M P L A T I O N

12

All the time we are talking to ourselves inside.
Yoga teaches, through meditation and practice,
that we should listen instead.

CONTEMPLATION

13

Yoga is where practice and
experience become one.

CONTEMPLATION

14

We know everything about everything
in this life, but we don't know ourselves.
The wise advise: know yourself, the Self.

CONTEMPLATION

_____

_____

_____

_____

15

Yoga means union—feeling the unity within.

CONTEMPLATION

_____

_____

_____

_____

16

Yogis do not feel that peace is dependent
on the outer world.

CONTEMPLATION

17

All yogic practices lead one
to the understanding of Self.

CONTEMPLATION

18

Yoga is a personal journey
that leads us to the universal.

CONTEMPLATION

_____

_____

_____

_____

III. Thirst

19

Coming into contact with what you are not,
makes you thirsty for what you Are.

CONTEMPLATION

_____

_____

_____

_____

20

Problems:
From problems, thirst arises. From thirst,
comes the impetus to practice. In this way,
a yogi sees problems as useful tools.

C O N T E M P L A T I O N

21

When you want something, everything moves
in that direction. So ask yourself what do I want?

CONTEMPLATION

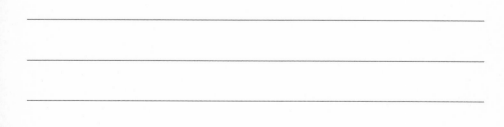

22

Thirst, which is attentive and not anxious,
is real *tṛṣṇā* thirst.

CONTEMPLATION

23

Thirst is like a guru, because
thirst guides us on the path.

CONTEMPLATION

_____

_____

_____

_____

24

When you lose what you want, do you have to
lose your equilibrium, as well?

C O N T E M P L A T I O N

_____

_____

_____

_____

25

Life experiences give us thirst for beingness.

C O N T E M P L A T I O N

_____

_____

_____

_____

26

The aim is to feel pure freedom.

CONTEMPLATION

_____

_____

_____

_____

27

Sometimes it takes a whole lot
of something to get to nothing.

CONTEMPLATION

_____

_____

_____

_____

IV. Guru

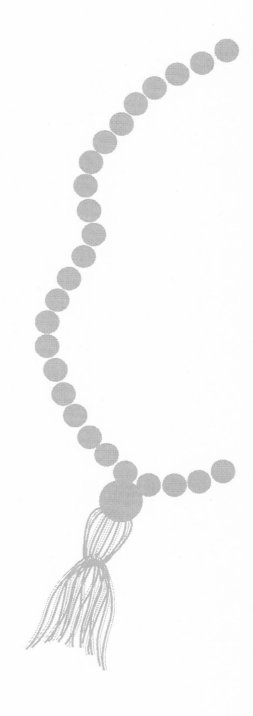

28

The Guru is one who enlightens you to something
you are not aware of, but you feel.

CONTEMPLATION

29

Guru is that light which leads
you to your own Self Awareness.

C O N T E M P L A T I O N

30

If you place your life at the feet of that light,
your life becomes that light.

CONTEMPLATION

_____

_____

_____

_____

31

The Guru exists as the manifest thread
that links one to the infinite.

CONTEMPLATION

_____

_____

_____

_____

32

It is a great thing to meet someone or something
that sparks the fire of Self Knowledge in you.

C O N T E M P L A T I O N

_____

_____

_____

_____

33

Some people are just giants of consciousness.

(Manorama Referring to Shri Brahmananda Sarasvati)

C O N T E M P L A T I O N

_____

_____

_____

_____

34

If we pay attention, everything is a Guru.

C O N T E M P L A T I O N

_____

_____

_____

_____

35

That in whom you find the end
of all things is your Sad Guru.

CONTEMPLATION

36

If we listen very carefully, Guru becomes
the pulsation of our own heart.

CONTEMPLATION

_____

_____

_____

_____

V. Mind

Mind is a good employee, not a good employer.

CONTEMPLATION

_____

_____

_____

_____

38

When we are involved with the
thinking mind alone, we crash. When we are
connected to the silent center we fly.

CONTEMPLATION

39

What is safer than a quiet mind?

CONTEMPLATION

_____

_____

_____

_____

40

How do we sit with silence when
the mind always wants to know so much?

CONTEMPLATION

When the mind can't find the answer to the why,
then you have the opportunity to go beyond
the mind. In this way, the UNANSWERABLE WHY
becomes a cosmic doorway that leads beyond
the level of the thinking mind.

CONTEMPLATION

42

Where the mind can't go ...
There is the entry point... There is the blessing.

CONTEMPLATION

43

You have to find the source of the mind.

C O N T E M P L A T I O N

_____

_____

_____

_____

44

Mind is always in the past or the future,
never in the present. Bring your attention
to the present and watch the play.

CONTEMPLATION

45

Don't buy what the mind is selling.

CONTEMPLATION

_____

_____

_____

_____

VI. Sanskrit

46

How does sound lead us to the silent mind,
and how does contact with silence bring
us to profound happiness?

CONTEMPLATION

_____

_____

_____

_____

47

Sanskrit awakens us to our essential pulsation.
Pulsation is always healing, because
it links us to the universal.

CONTEMPLATION

_____

_____

_____

_____

48

Sound is a doorway to everything because
everything in manifestation is made of vibration.

CONTEMPLATION

_____

_____

_____

_____

49

To come into contact with pure vibration
is to experience vast space.

CONTEMPLATION

50

Learning to entrain with a language of vibration,
like Sanskrit, helps us connect with
what we really are, vibration itself.

CONTEMPLATION

51

The balance in mantra is this:
The more energized the sound is,
the quieter the mind becomes by it.

C O N T E M P L A T I O N

52

However much silence you feel behind the
sound; that is how much *shakti* that sound has.

CONTEMPLATION

53

Sanskrit is the language of the eternal.
It is the language of Yoga.

54

OM is the ground underneath you.
OM is what all mantra springs from.
OM is the question Who am I?
And OM is the answer I AM.

C O N T E M P L A T I O N

Sanskrit

VII. Prana

55

The conscious engagement of sound
is the conscious engagement of breath.

CONTEMPLATION

_____

_____

56

Follow the *prana* because the *prana* is the force
that links us to the infinite.

CONTEMPLATION

_____

_____

_____

_____

57

Go where the *prana* opens up and you
will be happy. Go where it does not and you
will be fighting against the energy all the time.

CONTEMPLATION

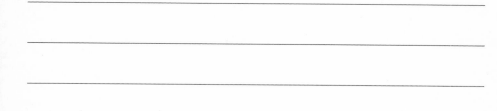

58

Proper engagement of *prana* is maturity.

CONTEMPLATION

59

Observe through conscious breathing
the relationship that exists
between the atmosphere and the body.

CONTEMPLATION

_____

_____

_____

_____

60

The more deeply we move into the practice,
the more we move into
the subtle aspect of the breath.

C O N T E M P L A T I O N

_____

_____

_____

_____

61

Breath is a doorway to experience the Self.

C O N T E M P L A T I O N

_____

_____

_____

_____

62

In Sanskrit, we learn to feel the breath,
to feel the *prana*.

CONTEMPLATION

63

Breath is never boring.

CONTEMPLATION

_____

_____

_____

_____

VIII. Mantra

64

Mantras allow us a chance to rest in sound.

CONTEMPLATION

_____

_____

_____

_____

65

Mantras quiet the mind by engaging sound
and breath in a harmonious way.

C O N T E M P L A T I O N

_____

_____

_____

_____

66

First thing to do before you chant is to connect
with the breath. First study the mantrik language,
then see how that language has a relationship
with the one who engages it.

CONTEMPLATION

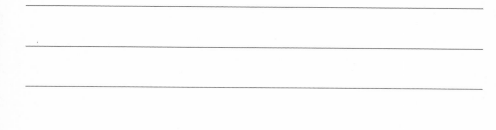

67

Rhythm brings clarity: through harmony of breath
and divine organization.

CONTEMPLATION

68

You must find your inner mantra before the outer
mantra can have deeper meaning.

CONTEMPLATION

_____

_____

_____

_____

69

Mantra's aim is for us to experience THAT.

C O N T E M P L A T I O N

70

When we practice chanting mantras; through repetition, we become One with the mantra.

CONTEMPLATION

_____

_____

_____

_____

71

When you let the mantra chant you, then
you understand the eternal OM.

CONTEMPLATION

_____

_____

_____

_____

72

All mantras resolve back to silence.

C O N T E M P L A T I O N

‑‑

‑‑

‑‑

IX. Knowledge

73

You are the only one going all the way with you in this life. So it's best to get to know your Self.

CONTEMPLATION

_____

_____

_____

_____

74

There is no *knowing* yoga, only being
with a state of yoga that is
what the wise mean when they say *knowing*.

CONTEMPLATION

75

There's no way you can swallow an ocean,
but you can learn to swim in it.
Sanskrit, is like an ocean.

CONTEMPLATION

76

Life is our learning ground.
We need to be fearless in this life.

CONTEMPLATION

You can fake a lot of things in life, but
you cannot fake knowing yourself to your Self.

CONTEMPLATION

_____

_____

_____

_____

Knowledge

78

You stay close to the union and
the union stays close to you.

C O N T E M P L A T I O N

_____

_____

_____

_____

79

Use knowledge to get you to feeling.

CONTEMPLATION

_____

_____

_____

_____

80

Knowledge helps us bridge the known
to the unknown. Then
we can experience the One known.

C O N T E M P L A T I O N

81

The key is to grasp the essence.

CONTEMPLATION

_____

_____

_____

_____

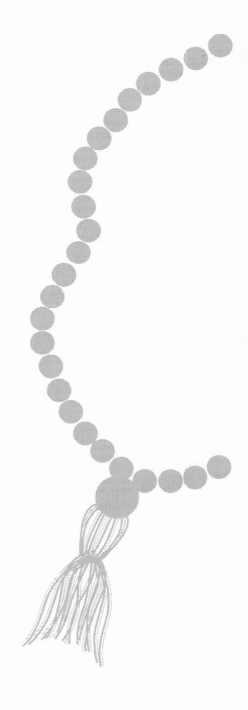

X. Awareness

The biggest question is the one least asked:
Who am I?

CONTEMPLATION

_____

_____

_____

_____

The real starting point of yoga is:
I don't know who I am.

CONTEMPLATION

_____

_____

_____

_____

84

When we admit where we are,
there consciousness begins.

C O N T E M P L A T I O N

_____

_____

_____

_____

It is very important to find out where
your attention is, because your attention
will tell you what you love.

CONTEMPLATION

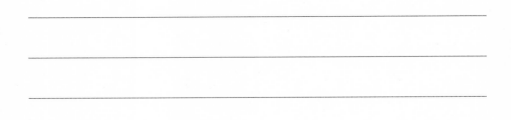

86

You have to see the other side to see something
fully. Otherwise, you haven't seen it at all.

CONTEMPLATION

_____

_____

_____

_____

87

We will make great strides if we go in and sit
with the fullness and the emptiness,
and learn to live with our aloneness.

C O N T E M P L A T I O N

_____

_____

_____

_____

88

We are not afraid of our smallness.
We're afraid of our vastness.

CONTEMPLATION

_____

_____

_____

_____

89

When you entrain with something,
you align with it.

CONTEMPLATION

90

Whether or not you call it Yoga,
awareness is the only way out.
How you get to awareness is your way out.

CONTEMPLATION

_____

_____

_____

_____

XI. Transformation

91

Feeling Is the transformation.

C O N T E M P L A T I O N

_____

- -

- -

- -

92

The essential ingredient in the transformative
process is love—Self-love.

CONTEMPLATION

_____

_____

_____

_____

93

We get a mixed bag in life.
Then we have to raise ourselves.

C O N T E M P L A T I O N

_____

_____

_____

_____

94

You always want to go to the root. Otherwise
you don't know what you are transforming.

CONTEMPLATION

_____

_____

_____

_____

95

When we connect with the universal,
we ourselves become the entry point.

CONTEMPLATION

_____

_____

_____

_____

96

With reverence comes love and grace.
With love and grace we feel
a great awakening in consciousness.

CONTEMPLATION

97

Awareness is the key factor in any transformation.

How do you know you have transformed?
You feel it.

CONTEMPLATION

98

Yoga will always ask you for what you are not.

C O N T E M P L A T I O N

99

It's a patient journey.

C O N T E M P L A T I O N

_____

_____

_____

_____

XII. Silence

100

Yogic silence:
In Yoga, silence is not just the
absence of speaking. Yogic silence
arises when we do not think.

CONTEMPLATION

101

If we listen carefully, we will hear that
sounds have silences and silences have sounds.

CONTEMPLATION

_____

_____

_____

_____

102

All the time we are talking to ourselves. Instead, we should spend more time listening to our Self.

CONTEMPLATION

_____

_____

_____

_____

103

If you want to get to the center, you have
to sit still and watch the movement.

CONTEMPLATION

104

When the mind is silent,
everything is properly understood.

C O N T E M P L A T I O N

_____

_____

_____

_____

105

We need to be able to sit with our chatter,
our confusion, in order to find clarity,
understanding and stillness.

CONTEMPLATION

106

What is the ultimate, original thought, but I AM.
Beyond that is experience itself.

C O N T E M P L A T I O N

107

Silence is the highest expression of love.

CONTEMPLATION

108

The ultimate language of Self
is silence and feeling.

C O N T E M P L A T I O N

_____

_____

_____

_____

BIOGRAPHY OF THE AUTHOR

Manorama lives in New York City. She travels throughout the world, leading workshops on Yoga, Meditation and Sanskrit, as the Path of Luminous Shabda. She has been featured on numerous CD's. This is her first book.

For more info on Manorama & Sanskrit Studies visit
www.sanskritstudies.org

INDEX OF WORDS AND TERMS

Sanskrit – Original language of Yoga.

Prana – Breath, Energy, Life force.

OM – A mantra. The shortest way to say the supreme Self. The cycle of being, and becoming, and beyond. Silent pulsation.

Guru – Teacher, Remover of darkness, Light.

Sad-Guru – Supreme guide stationed in beingness. Supreme light.

Karma – Action

Mantra – Sacred sounds united to protect the mind and heart.

Yoga – Union. Experience of Wholeness.

I-AM – Term that Shri Brahmananda Sarasvati used to describe beingness or the Self.

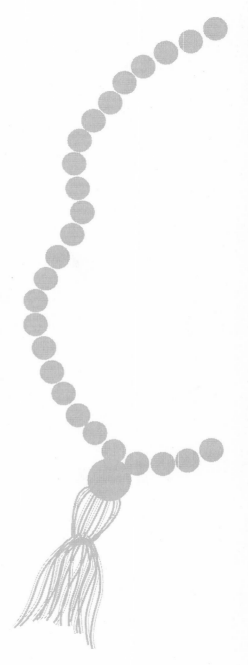

Thread of Wisdom
Yoga Pearls
VOLUME 1
WITH MANORAMA

SANSKRIT STUDIES

Luminous Shabda Press, New York
Printed in the United States of America
Library of Congress
ISBN # 978-0-578-02772-2

All Yoga Pearls by Manorama
Editor Jennafer D'Alvia
Author photo by James Ferrara
Design by Naked Design

TABLE OF CONTENTS

I.   Reverence

II.   Yoga

III.   Thirst

IV.   Guru

V.   Mind

VI.   Sanskrit

VII.   Prana

VIII. Mantra

IX.   Knowledge

X.   Awareness

XI.   Transformation

XII.   Silence